Breakthrough Strategies: Unleashing Innovation and Disruption for Business Success

Contents,

Introduction

Intro

In today's rapidly evolving business landscape, staying ahead of the competition requires more than just incremental improvements or minor adjustments. It demands a mindset of innovation and the ability to disrupt existing norms and practices. Organizations that can unleash the power of breakthrough strategies have the potential to reshape industries, redefine customer expectations, and achieve extraordinary success. This book serves as a guide to help businesses embrace innovation, navigate disruption, and unlock their full potential for sustainable growth.

The Power of Breakthrough Strategies:

Breakthrough strategies represent a departure from traditional approaches to business. Instead of incremental change, they involve radical shifts in thinking, vision, and execution. These strategies are centred around innovative ideas, disruptive technologies, and creative approaches to delivering value to customers. They challenge the status quo, challenge conventional wisdom, and drive transformation on a profound level.

Unleashing Innovation:

Innovation lies at the heart of breakthrough strategies. It is the catalyst that sparks new ideas, fosters creativity, and propels organizations forward. By embracing innovation, businesses can identify untapped opportunities, develop ground-breaking products and services, and create unique value propositions that set them apart from competitors. Innovation is not limited to product development; it encompasses all aspects of the business, including processes, business models, marketing strategies, and customer experiences.

Navigating Disruption:

In today's hyperconnected and rapidly changing world, disruption has become a constant force. Technological advancements, shifting consumer preferences, and evolving market dynamics are reshaping industries at an unprecedented pace. Organizations that can navigate disruption effectively can capitalize on emerging trends, adapt to changing circumstances, and seize new opportunities. By proactively embracing disruption, businesses can turn threats into opportunities and position themselves as market leaders.

The Path to Business Success:

Breakthrough strategies pave the way for business success by driving innovation, fostering agility, and embracing change. They empower organizations to challenge conventional wisdom, take calculated risks, and explore uncharted territories. However, achieving success in this realm requires a holistic approach that encompasses various key elements.

Firstly, a culture of innovation must be fostered within the organization. This involves creating an environment that encourages and rewards creativity, curiosity, and experimentation. It requires leadership support, open communication channels, and a willingness to learn from both successes and failures. An innovative culture empowers employees at all levels to contribute ideas, challenge assumptions, and drive change.

Secondly, organizations must develop a deep understanding of their customers and their evolving needs. Customer-centricity is essential for designing breakthrough strategies that resonate with target audiences. By leveraging data, customer insights, and design thinking principles, businesses can develop products, services, and experiences that exceed customer expectations and create long-term loyalty.

Thirdly, a strategic focus on technology and emerging trends is crucial. Breakthrough strategies often leverage cutting-edge technologies, such as artificial intelligence, blockchain, Internet of Things (IoT), and data analytics. Organizations need to stay abreast of technological advancements, identify relevant opportunities, and align their business strategies accordingly. By harnessing technology, businesses can streamline operations, enhance efficiency, and deliver innovative solutions to customers.

Moreover, collaboration and partnerships play a vital role in breakthrough strategies. In today's interconnected world, no organization can thrive in isolation. Collaborative networks, strategic alliances, and ecosystem partnerships enable businesses to access diverse expertise, leverage complementary resources, and drive collective innovation. Collaboration also fosters a broader perspective, accelerates learning, and expands market reach.

Lastly, continuous learning, adaptability, and agility are essential to sustaining breakthrough strategies. Organizations must have the capacity to pivot, iterate, and respond swiftly to changing market conditions. This requires a willingness to challenge the status quo, embrace ambiguity, and make informed decisions based on data and insights.

Breakthrough strategies hold the key to unlocking the full potential of organizations in today's dynamic and competitive business landscape. By embracing innovation, navigating disruption, and adopting a holistic approach, businesses can position themselves for long-term success.

This book, "Breakthrough Strategies: Unleashing Innovation and Disruption for Business Success," is designed to provide readers with a comprehensive understanding of the principles, practices, and frameworks necessary to drive breakthrough strategies within their organizations. It delves into the mindset of innovation, explores the dynamics of disruption, and offers practical insights and strategies to navigate the complexities of the business environment.

Throughout the chapters, readers will gain valuable insights into fostering a culture of innovation, harnessing emerging technologies, developing customer-centric approaches, and cultivating collaboration and partnerships. The book will also address the challenges and opportunities associated with navigating disruption and provide guidance on adapting to changing market conditions.

By drawing on real-world examples, case studies, and expert perspectives, this book aims to inspire readers to think differently, challenge existing paradigms, and embrace a mindset of continuous improvement and growth. It encourages readers to explore uncharted territories, experiment with new ideas, and take calculated risks to achieve breakthrough results.

Whether readers are seasoned executives, entrepreneurs, or aspiring business leaders, this book serves as a roadmap for driving innovation, navigating disruption, and achieving sustainable business success. It provides practical frameworks, actionable strategies, and thought-provoking insights to guide readers on their journey toward unleashing the power of breakthrough strategies.

The business landscape is evolving at an unprecedented pace, presenting both challenges and opportunities for organizations. By embracing innovation and disruption, businesses can position themselves as market leaders and drive sustainable growth. "Breakthrough Strategies: Unleashing Innovation and Disruption for Business Success" serves as a valuable resource for individuals and organizations seeking to thrive in this dynamic environment. By leveraging the insights and strategies presented in this book, readers will be equipped to navigate the complexities of the business landscape, embrace change, and unleash the transformative power of breakthrough strategies.

Chapter 1: The Power of Innovation: Driving Business Transformation

Innovation has long been recognized as a critical driver of business success and growth. It has the power to transform industries, disrupt established markets, and propel organizations to new heights. In today's dynamic and competitive business landscape, the ability to harness the power of innovation is more important than ever. This article explores the significance of innovation in driving business transformation and outlines key strategies for organizations to unleash its power.

Innovation as a Catalyst for Transformation:

Innovation is not simply about coming up with new ideas or creating novel products. It encompasses a broader mindset and approach that challenges the status quo, questions existing practices, and seeks to find better ways of doing things. Innovation is a catalyst for transformation because it enables organizations to reimagine their business models, processes, and strategies. It encourages a culture of continuous improvement and adaptation, allowing businesses to stay relevant and competitive in an ever-changing environment.

Business transformation driven by innovation involves making fundamental changes to the way an organization operates, thinks, and delivers value to customers. It requires a willingness to take risks, experiment with new ideas, and embrace failure as a learning opportunity. By fostering a culture of innovation, organizations create an environment where employees are empowered to think creatively, challenge assumptions, and contribute to the transformational journey.

The Benefits of Innovation-Driven Transformation:

Embracing innovation as a driver of business transformation offers numerous benefits to organizations:

Competitive Advantage: Innovation enables organizations to differentiate themselves from competitors. By introducing unique products, services, or business models, businesses can capture market share, attract new customers, and strengthen customer loyalty.

Increased Efficiency and Productivity: Innovation often leads to improved processes, technologies, and workflows, resulting in enhanced efficiency and productivity. By embracing automation, optimization, and digitalization, organizations can streamline operations, reduce costs, and free up resources for other strategic initiatives.

Enhanced Customer Experience: Innovation-driven transformation allows organizations to better understand customer needs and preferences, leading to the development of tailored products and services. By offering personalized experiences, organizations can create strong emotional connections with customers and drive customer loyalty and advocacy.

Adaptation to Market Changes: Innovation enables organizations to adapt to evolving market conditions. By constantly monitoring trends, anticipating disruptions, and embracing change, businesses can proactively respond to emerging opportunities and challenges, positioning themselves as agile and resilient players in their industries.

Attraction and Retention of Talent: Organizations that foster a culture of innovation are more likely to attract and retain top talent. Innovative companies are seen as exciting and dynamic places to work, providing employees with opportunities for growth, learning, and impactful work.

Strategies for Unleashing the Power of Innovation:

To drive business transformation through innovation, organizations can adopt the following strategies:

Foster a Culture of Innovation: Building an innovation-driven culture starts with leadership commitment and setting the tone from the top. Organizations should encourage and reward creativity, risk-taking, and collaboration. They should provide employees with the freedom to experiment, learn from failure, and share ideas. Creating cross-functional innovation teams and establishing dedicated innovation programs can also promote a culture that nurtures and supports innovative thinking.

Encourage Collaboration and Diversity: Innovation thrives in an environment that encourages collaboration and embraces diverse perspectives. Organizations should foster interdisciplinary collaboration, break down silos, and encourage open dialogue. By bringing together individuals with different backgrounds, skills, and perspectives, organizations can foster creativity, spark new ideas, and drive breakthrough innovation.

Invest in Research and Development: Allocating resources to research and development (R&D) activities is crucial for driving innovation. Organizations should invest in exploring emerging technologies, conducting market research, and staying abreast of industry trends. R&D efforts should be aligned with the organization's strategic goals and priorities, focusing on areas that have the

potential to drive significant business impact and create value for customers.

Embrace Customer-Centricity: Putting the customer at the center of innovation efforts is essential for driving business transformation. Organizations should invest in understanding customer needs, preferences, and pain points through research, feedback loops, and data analytics. By incorporating customer insights into the innovation process, businesses can develop solutions that address real-world problems and deliver exceptional customer experiences.

Encourage Experimentation and Learning: Innovation involves taking risks and learning from both successes and failures. Organizations should create a safe space for experimentation, where employees are encouraged to test new ideas, pilot projects, and iterate based on feedback. Embracing a "fail fast, learn fast" mentality enables organizations to quickly adapt and refine their innovations, increasing the likelihood of success in the long run.

Foster External Partnerships: Collaboration with external partners, such as startups, research institutions, and industry experts, can accelerate innovation and drive business transformation. Organizations should actively seek opportunities for partnerships and collaborations to access new technologies, knowledge, and resources. Strategic alliances, joint ventures, and open innovation initiatives can bring fresh perspectives and expand the organization's capabilities.

Empower and Support Innovation Champions: Identifying and empowering innovation champions within the organization is vital for driving innovation-led transformation. These individuals can serve as catalysts, inspiring and mobilizing teams to embrace innovation and challenge the status quo. Organizations should provide them with the necessary support, resources, and platforms to champion and implement innovative ideas.

Create a Framework for Innovation: Establishing a structured framework for managing innovation initiatives is critical for driving business transformation. This framework should include clear processes, metrics, and governance mechanisms to guide the innovation journey. It should align with the organization's strategic goals, provide a systematic approach to idea generation and evaluation, and ensure effective implementation of innovative solutions.

The power of innovation to drive business transformation cannot be overstated. Organizations that embrace innovation as a strategic imperative and create an environment conducive to creativity, collaboration, and experimentation are better positioned to thrive in today's rapidly changing business landscape. By fostering a culture of innovation, investing in research and development, embracing customer-centricity, and fostering external partnerships, organizations can unleash the full potential of innovation to drive transformative change. With the right strategies and a relentless focus on innovation, organizations can navigate disruptions, outpace competitors, and achieve sustainable success in the dynamic and evolving marketplace.

Chapter 2: Embracing Disruption: Navigating Industry Shifts and Trends

In today's fast-paced and ever-evolving business landscape, industries are experiencing constant shifts and disruptions. Technological advancements, changing consumer behaviours, and emerging market trends are reshaping traditional business models and challenging the status quo. To thrive in this environment, organizations must embrace disruption rather than resist it. Chapter 2 of this book, titled "Embracing Disruption: Navigating Industry Shifts and Trends," explores the importance of recognizing and adapting to these shifts, and provides strategies for successfully navigating the turbulent waters of industry disruption.

Understanding Industry Shifts and Trends:

Industry shifts and trends are transformative forces that significantly impact businesses. They can arise from various sources, such as advancements in technology, changes in consumer preferences, regulatory developments, or global economic shifts. By recognizing and understanding these shifts and trends, organizations can proactively respond to them, stay ahead of the competition, and capitalize on emerging opportunities.

Navigating Disruption:

Disruption can be seen as both a threat and an opportunity. It challenges existing business models, products, and practices, but it also opens doors for innovation, growth, and market leadership. Navigating disruption requires a strategic approach that involves:

Continuous Monitoring: Organizations must actively monitor their industry and the broader business environment for signs of disruption. This involves staying informed about technological advancements, market trends, competitor activities, and changing customer behaviours. By keeping a pulse on the industry, organizations can anticipate disruptions and adjust their strategies accordingly.

Agility and Flexibility: In the face of disruption, organizations must be agile and adaptable. They should have the flexibility to pivot their strategies, business models, and operations to align with new market dynamics. This may involve making quick decisions, reallocating resources, and embracing experimentation to test new approaches and ideas.

Embracing Innovation: Disruption often stems from innovative ideas, technologies, or business models. To navigate industry shifts and trends, organizations must foster a culture of innovation. This includes encouraging employees to think creatively, explore new possibilities, and challenge conventional thinking. By fostering innovation, organizations can identify novel solutions, create competitive advantages, and lead the market.

Collaborative Networks: Collaboration and partnerships can be powerful tools for navigating disruption. Organizations should seek opportunities to collaborate with startups, industry peers, research institutions, and other stakeholders. Collaborative networks provide access to diverse expertise, resources, and new perspectives, enabling organizations to jointly explore emerging opportunities and address shared challenges.

Customer-Centric Approach: Disruption often brings changes in customer expectations and behaviours. Organizations must understand these shifts and align their strategies with customer needs and preferences. By embracing a customer-centric approach, organizations can develop innovative products, services, and experiences that meet evolving demands and drive customer loyalty.

Talent and Skills Development: Navigating disruption requires a workforce equipped with the right skills and mindset. Organizations must invest in talent development, reskilling, and upskilling initiatives to ensure their employees are prepared for the challenges and opportunities brought about by industry shifts. This may involve fostering a learning culture, providing training programs, and attracting talent with diverse backgrounds and expertise.

Strategic Partnerships and Investments: To navigate disruption, organizations should consider strategic partnerships and investments in emerging technologies, startups, or disruptive ventures. By collaborating with or investing in innovative companies, organizations can gain access to new capabilities, expand their offerings, and stay at the forefront of industry developments.

Chapter 3: Building a Culture of Innovation: Fostering Creativity and Risk-Taking

Innovation has become a key driver of success and competitive advantage in today's rapidly evolving business landscape. Organizations that foster a culture of innovation are better positioned to adapt to change, anticipate market trends, and deliver value to customers. Building a culture of innovation requires creating an environment that encourages and nurtures creativity, experimentation, and risk-taking. In this chapter, we delve into the importance of building a culture of innovation and provide strategies for fostering creativity and risk-taking within organizations.

The Importance of a Culture of Innovation:

A culture of innovation is a set of values, behaviours, and practices that encourages and supports the generation and implementation of new ideas. It empowers employees at all levels to think differently, challenge the status quo, and contribute to the organization's growth and success. Here are key reasons why building a culture of innovation is vital:

Competitive Advantage: In today's dynamic business landscape, organizations need to differentiate themselves to stay ahead of the competition. A culture of innovation enables businesses to develop unique products, services, and solutions that meet evolving customer needs and outperform competitors.

Adaptability and Agility: Innovation thrives in organizations that are agile and adaptable. A culture of innovation encourages employees to embrace change, experiment with new ideas, and adapt quickly to market shifts. It enables organizations to respond effectively to disruptions and seize emerging opportunities.

Employee Engagement and Retention: An innovative culture fosters a sense of purpose and engagement among employees. When individuals are encouraged to contribute their ideas and see them implemented, they feel valued and motivated. This, in turn, enhances employee retention and attracts top talent.

Continuous Improvement: Innovation is not limited to ground-breaking inventions. It also involves incremental improvements and process optimization. A culture of innovation promotes a mindset of continuous improvement, driving efficiency, productivity, and quality across the organization.

Strategies for Fostering Creativity and Risk-Taking:

Building a culture of innovation requires a deliberate and strategic approach. Here are strategies organizations can employ to foster creativity and risk-taking:

Leadership Support: Innovation starts at the top. Leaders need to demonstrate their commitment to innovation by setting clear expectations, providing resources, and actively participating in innovation initiatives. Leaders should also communicate the importance of creativity and risk-taking, emphasizing that failure is a valuable learning opportunity.

Create Psychological Safety: To foster creativity, organizations must create an environment where employees feel safe to express their ideas and opinions without fear of judgment or reprisal. Psychological safety encourages open dialogue, constructive feedback, and a willingness to take risks.

Encourage Diverse Perspectives: Innovation thrives when there is a diversity of perspectives and ideas. Organizations should embrace diversity in all its forms, including gender, race, age, and background. By fostering an inclusive environment, organizations can tap into a wide range of viewpoints and experiences, sparking creativity and driving innovation.

Provide Resources and Tools: Innovation requires the necessary resources and tools to turn ideas into reality. Organizations should allocate dedicated resources, such as time, funding, and technology, to support innovation initiatives. This can include creating innovation labs, providing access to prototyping facilities, and offering training programs on creative thinking and problem-solving.

Embrace Collaboration: Collaboration is a powerful catalyst for innovation. Encourage cross-functional collaboration and create opportunities for employees to collaborate on projects and share ideas. Foster a culture of teamwork and create platforms for collaboration, such as innovation workshops, brainstorming sessions, and cross-departmental projects.

Reward and Recognize Innovation: Recognizing and rewarding innovative efforts motivates employees to contribute their ideas. Organizations should establish formal mechanisms to acknowledge and reward innovative thinking and successful implementations. This can include performance incentives, innovation awards, or recognition programs.

Emphasize Learning and Development: Continuous learning and development are essential for fostering a culture of innovation. Organizations should invest in training programs that enhance creativity, problem-solving, and entrepreneurial skills. Encourage employees to pursue personal and professional growth by providing access to learning resources, workshops, and conferences related to innovation and emerging trends.

Celebrate Failure as a Learning Opportunity: In a culture of innovation, failure is not seen as a setback but as a stepping stone to success. Encourage a growth mindset where failure is embraced as a valuable learning opportunity. Share stories of failed experiments and the lessons learned from them. This helps create a safe environment where employees feel comfortable taking calculated risks.

Establish Innovation Champions: Identify and empower individuals within the organization who are passionate about innovation. These innovation champions can serve as catalysts, inspiring and guiding others in the pursuit of innovative ideas. Provide them with the autonomy and resources to drive innovation initiatives and share their knowledge and experiences with the broader organization.

Measure and Track Innovation: To foster a culture of innovation, organizations need to measure and track innovation efforts. Establish key performance indicators (KPIs) related to innovation, such as the number of ideas generated, successful implementations, or revenue generated from new products or services. Regularly review and communicate progress to create accountability and drive continuous improvement.

Building a culture of innovation is a strategic imperative for organizations seeking to thrive in today's dynamic and competitive business environment. By fostering creativity, risk-taking, collaboration, and continuous learning, organizations can unleash the full potential of their employees and drive sustainable innovation. Embracing a culture of innovation not only leads to new products, services, and processes but also cultivates an environment of engagement, adaptability, and resilience. Through the implementation of these strategies, organizations can position themselves as leaders in their industries, continuously evolve to meet customer needs, and navigate industry shifts and disruptions with confidence.

Chapter 4: Harnessing Emerging Technologies: Exploring the Frontiers of Innovation

Emerging technologies have the power to revolutionize industries, disrupt traditional business models, and unlock new possibilities for innovation. From artificial intelligence and machine learning to blockchain, Internet of Things (IoT), and virtual reality, these technologies present exciting opportunities for organizations to push the boundaries of what is possible. In this chapter, we delve into the topic of harnessing emerging technologies and explore how organizations can leverage them to drive innovation and stay ahead in the competitive landscape.

The Power of Emerging Technologies:

Emerging technologies are transformative forces that have the potential to reshape industries and create entirely new business opportunities. They offer organizations the ability to automate processes, enhance customer experiences, improve operational efficiency, and gain valuable insights from data. Here are key reasons why harnessing emerging technologies is crucial for innovation:

Disruption and Competitive Advantage: Organizations that embrace emerging technologies can disrupt their industries and gain a competitive edge. By leveraging these technologies to develop new products, services, or business models, organizations can differentiate themselves and capture market share in dynamic and rapidly evolving markets.

Enhanced Customer Experiences: Emerging technologies enable organizations to create immersive and personalized customer experiences. By leveraging technologies like virtual reality, augmented reality, or chatbots, organizations can engage customers in innovative ways, deliver tailored solutions, and provide seamless interactions across multiple channels.

Improved Operational Efficiency: Emerging technologies offer organizations the opportunity to streamline and automate their operations, leading to improved efficiency and cost savings. For example, the use of artificial intelligence and robotic process automation can optimize repetitive tasks, reduce errors, and free up resources for more strategic initiatives.

Data-Driven Decision Making: Emerging technologies provide organizations with advanced analytics and data processing capabilities. By harnessing the power of big data, machine learning, and predictive analytics, organizations can extract valuable insights, identify trends, and make data-driven decisions that drive innovation and business growth.

Agility and Adaptability: Organizations that embrace emerging technologies are better equipped to adapt to changing market conditions. These technologies enable organizations to be more agile, responsive, and flexible in meeting customer demands and navigating industry shifts. They provide the tools to rapidly prototype, iterate, and pivot strategies based on real-time feedback and insights.

Strategies for Harnessing Emerging Technologies:

To effectively harness emerging technologies and drive innovation, organizations should consider the following strategies:

Stay Informed and Continuously Learn: Emerging technologies evolve rapidly, and it's crucial for organizations to stay informed about the latest developments. Establish mechanisms to monitor technology trends, attend industry conferences, participate in communities of practice, and engage with experts and thought leaders. Continuous learning ensures organizations remain at the forefront of technological advancements.

Conduct Technology Scans and Assessments: Regularly assess emerging technologies to identify their potential impact on the organization. Conduct technology scans to evaluate the maturity, feasibility, and applicability of different technologies. This assessment helps organizations prioritize investments, allocate resources, and determine which technologies align best with their business objectives and innovation goals.

Foster a Culture of Experimentation: Innovation requires a willingness to experiment and take calculated risks. Encourage employees to explore emerging technologies, experiment with prototypes, and test new ideas. Create a safe environment where failure is seen as a learning opportunity, and successes are celebrated. Establish dedicated innovation labs or sandboxes where teams can experiment and collaborate.

Cultivate Partnerships and Collaborations: Collaboration is key when it comes to harnessing emerging technologies. Organizations should seek partnerships with technology vendors, startups, research institutions, and industry peers. Collaborations provide access to expertise, resources, and shared knowledge, accelerating the adoption and implementation of emerging technologies.

Develop an Innovation Roadmap: Create a clear roadmap that outlines how emerging technologies will be integrated into the organization's innovation strategy. Identify the key areas or use cases where emerging technologies can have the most significant impact. Prioritize these areas based on their alignment with business goals, customer needs, and market opportunities. The innovation roadmap should outline the timeline, resources required, and milestones for implementing and leveraging emerging technologies.

Build a Cross-Functional Innovation Team: Establish a dedicated team or innovation task force that brings together individuals from different departments and disciplines. This team should have a deep understanding of emerging technologies and their potential applications within the organization. By fostering collaboration and cross-functional expertise, organizations can effectively explore, pilot, and scale emerging technologies.

Invest in Talent and Skill Development: To harness emerging technologies, organizations need talent equipped with the necessary skills and knowledge. Invest in training programs and initiatives that upskill employees in areas such as data analytics, artificial intelligence, cybersecurity, and user experience design. Encourage employees to pursue certifications and external learning opportunities to stay abreast of the latest developments in emerging technologies.

Develop a Data Strategy: Emerging technologies rely on data as their fuel. Organizations should develop a comprehensive data strategy that encompasses data collection, storage, integration, analysis, and governance. Ensure data privacy and security measures are in place to protect sensitive information. Implement data-driven processes and technologies to leverage the full potential of emerging technologies in generating actionable insights.

Pilot and Iterate: Start small by piloting emerging technologies in specific use cases or areas of the business. This allows organizations to assess their effectiveness, identify challenges, and make necessary adjustments. Encourage a culture of iteration and continuous improvement, where feedback from pilot initiatives is used to refine strategies and ensure successful implementation.

Monitor and Evaluate: It's crucial to monitor the impact and ROI of harnessing emerging technologies. Define key performance indicators (KPIs) that align with the organization's goals and track progress regularly. Monitor user feedback, customer satisfaction, operational efficiencies, and other relevant metrics to evaluate the success of implementing emerging technologies. Use these insights to refine strategies, make informed decisions, and drive further innovation.

Harnessing emerging technologies is a vital component of driving innovation and staying ahead in today's fast-paced business landscape. By embracing these technologies, organizations can unlock new opportunities, enhance customer experiences, improve operational efficiencies, and gain a competitive advantage. However, successful implementation requires a strategic approach, including staying informed, fostering a culture of experimentation, cultivating collaborations, and investing in talent and skill development. By following these strategies and adapting them to their specific contexts, organizations can effectively harness the frontiers of innovation and position themselves as leaders in their industries.

Chapter 5: Design Thinking: Putting the Customer at the Heart of Innovation

Innovation is a powerful driver of business success, but its true impact lies in the value it creates for customers. Organizations that prioritize customer-centric innovation have a greater chance of achieving sustainable growth and gaining a competitive edge. In this chapter, we explore the importance of putting the customer at the heart of innovation and discuss strategies for designing and delivering solutions that meet their evolving needs.

Understanding Customer Needs:

To truly put the customer at the heart of innovation, organizations must have a deep understanding of their needs, pain points, and aspirations. This understanding goes beyond surface-level demographics and extends to a comprehensive understanding of their desires, motivations, and behaviours. Here are key strategies for gaining insights into customer needs:

Conduct Market Research: Use market research techniques such as surveys, interviews, focus groups, and observation to gather data on customer preferences, expectations, and challenges. This research helps organizations identify gaps in the market and uncover unmet needs that can be addressed through innovative solutions.

Leverage Customer Feedback: Actively seek and incorporate customer feedback at every stage of the innovation process. Engage customers through feedback channels, social media, customer support interactions, and user testing sessions. This feedback provides valuable insights into customer experiences, pain points, and desired improvements.

Analyse Customer Data: Utilize data analytics tools to analyse customer data, including purchase history, behaviour patterns, and engagement metrics. This data-driven approach helps uncover trends, identify opportunities for personalization, and make informed decisions about product development and enhancements.

Design Thinking and Empathy:

Design thinking is a human-centred approach that fosters empathy, encourages creativity, and drives innovation. By employing design thinking methodologies, organizations can better understand and address customer needs. Here's how design thinking can be applied to put the customer at the heart of innovation:

Empathize with Customers: Design thinking starts with empathizing with customers to gain a deep understanding of their experiences and emotions. Engage in ethnographic research, conduct user interviews, and immerse yourself in their world to uncover insights that inform innovative solutions.

Define the Problem: Clearly define the problem or opportunity based on customer insights. Focus on understanding the underlying needs and motivations behind the challenges customers face. This ensures that the innovation efforts are aligned with solving real problems and meeting genuine customer needs.

Ideate and Prototype: Encourage cross-functional teams to brainstorm and generate a wide range of ideas to address the defined problem. Rapidly prototype and iterate on these ideas to test their feasibility and desirability. Involve customers in the co-creation process to validate and refine the concepts.

Test and Iterate: Continuously test and refine the prototypes based on customer feedback. Conduct user testing sessions and gather insights to make iterative improvements. This iterative approach ensures that the final solution is refined, intuitive, and truly resonates with customers.

Co-Creation and Collaboration:

Successful customer-centric innovation involves actively involving customers in the co-creation process. By collaborating with customers, organizations gain valuable insights, co-design solutions, and build stronger relationships. Here's how co-creation and collaboration can be fostered:

Engage in Customer Co-Creation: Invite customers to participate in the innovation process by seeking their input, ideas, and feedback. This can be done through customer advisory panels, beta testing programs, or online communities. Engaging customers as co-creators ensures that their perspectives and ideas are integrated into the final solution.

Foster Open Collaboration: Encourage collaboration and knowledge sharing among internal teams, external partners, and customers. Create platforms or digital spaces for open communication and collaboration, allowing diverse stakeholders to share insights, ideas, and expertise. This collaborative approach sparks creativity and generates innovative solutions.

Iterate Based on Customer Feedback: Continuously iterate based on customer feedback and insights gathered through co-creation activities. Regularly solicit feedback from customers and use it to refine and enhance the solutions. This ongoing collaboration ensures that the innovation efforts remain aligned with customer needs and preferences.

Build Long-Term Relationships: Engaging customers in the co-creation process fosters a sense of ownership and loyalty. By involving customers in the innovation journey, organizations can build strong, long-term relationships based on trust and mutual value. This customer-centric approach creates brand advocates who not only provide valuable feedback but also promote the organization's innovative solutions to others.

Adapting to Changing Customer Needs:

Putting the customer at the heart of innovation requires organizations to stay attuned to changing customer needs and evolving market trends. Here are strategies for adapting and staying responsive:

Continuous Customer Research: Conduct ongoing market research and gather real-time insights to stay updated on shifting customer needs, preferences, and behaviours. Regularly analyse customer data and feedback to identify emerging trends and patterns.

Agile Innovation Processes: Embrace agile methodologies to ensure flexibility and adaptability in the innovation process. Adopt iterative approaches that allow for rapid prototyping, testing, and refinement based on customer feedback. This agility enables organizations to respond quickly to changing customer needs and market dynamics.

Customer Journey Mapping: Map out the customer journey and identify touchpoints where innovation can enhance the overall experience. Understand the pain points, expectations, and moments of delight for customers. Use these insights to develop innovative solutions that create memorable experiences at every stage of the customer journey.

Embrace Emerging Technologies: Stay abreast of emerging technologies and their potential impact on customer experiences. Continuously explore how these technologies can be leveraged to enhance and personalize interactions with customers. From AI-powered chatbots to virtual reality experiences, integrating emerging technologies can provide unique and innovative ways to engage and delight customers.

Putting the customer at the heart of innovation is a fundamental principle for organizations striving to create sustainable growth and competitive advantage. By deeply understanding customer needs, leveraging design thinking methodologies, fostering co-creation and collaboration, and adapting to changing customer preferences, organizations can design and deliver innovative solutions that truly resonate with their target audience. This customer-centric approach not only drives business success but also fosters strong customer relationships and loyalty. By continuously listening to customers, involving them in the innovation process, and adapting to their evolving needs, organizations can position themselves as leaders in their industries and consistently deliver value that exceeds customer expectations.

Chapter 6: Agile Innovation: Adapting and Iterating for Rapid Progress

The Principles of Agile Innovation:

Embrace Iterative Processes: Agile innovation is characterized by a cycle of continuous iteration and improvement. Rather than pursuing lengthy and rigid development cycles, organizations break down projects into smaller, manageable increments. Each iteration involves developing a minimum viable product (MVP) or prototype, testing it, gathering feedback, and making necessary refinements. This iterative approach allows organizations to learn and adapt quickly, accelerating the pace of innovation.

Foster Cross-Functional Collaboration: Agile innovation thrives on cross-functional collaboration and shared ownership. It brings together individuals from different departments, disciplines, and backgrounds to work collaboratively on innovation initiatives. By fostering a culture of collaboration, organizations can leverage diverse perspectives, skills, and expertise to generate creative ideas and find innovative solutions.

Emphasize Customer Feedback: Agile innovation places a strong emphasis on gathering and incorporating customer feedback throughout the development process. Organizations actively engage with customers, seeking their input, and involving them in testing and validation. This customer-centric approach ensures that the solutions being developed truly meet customer needs, resulting in higher customer satisfaction and market relevance.

Embrace Flexibility and Adaptability: Agility is at the core of agile innovation. Organizations must be willing to embrace change, adapt quickly to new information, and adjust their course as needed. This flexibility allows them to respond to market shifts, emerging trends, and evolving customer preferences, ensuring that their innovation efforts remain aligned with changing dynamics.

Implementing Agile Innovation:

Create Cross-Functional Teams: Form cross-functional teams comprising individuals from different departments or disciplines who can contribute diverse perspectives and skills. These teams should be empowered to make decisions, collaborate closely, and take ownership of the innovation process. By bringing together a mix of talents and backgrounds, organizations can foster a culture of collaboration and creativity.

Adopt Agile Methodologies: Implement agile methodologies such as Scrum or Kanban to structure and manage innovation projects. These methodologies provide a framework for breaking down work into manageable tasks, setting priorities, and facilitating iterative development.

Agile methodologies also enable teams to track progress, identify bottlenecks, and make necessary adjustments in real-time.

Encourage Experimentation and Risk-Taking: Agile innovation thrives on experimentation and calculated risk-taking. Encourage teams to explore new ideas, test hypotheses, and take calculated risks in their pursuit of innovative solutions. Celebrate failures as learning opportunities and create a safe environment where individuals are encouraged to push boundaries and think outside the box.

Implement Rapid Prototyping: Develop prototypes or MVPs early in the innovation process to gather feedback and validate assumptions. Rapid prototyping allows organizations to test concepts, iterate quickly, and make informed decisions based on real-world user feedback. This iterative approach helps reduce the risk of investing resources in solutions that may not meet customer needs.

Leverage Agile Tools and Technologies: Utilize digital tools and technologies that support agile collaboration, project management, and communication. Agile project management software, virtual collaboration platforms, and communication tools facilitate seamless collaboration, transparency, and visibility across teams, especially in distributed or remote work environments.

Foster a Learning Culture: Encourage a culture of continuous learning and improvement. Encourage teams to reflect on their work, share learnings, and apply insights to future projects. Create opportunities for knowledge sharing, such as regular retrospectives, brown bag sessions, or internal workshops, where teams can discuss challenges, successes, and lessons learned. By fostering a learning culture, organizations can continuously improve their innovation practices and enhance their ability to adapt and iterate.

Benefits of Agile Innovation:

Increased Speed and Time-to-Market: Agile innovation allows organizations to bring new ideas to market faster. By breaking down projects into smaller iterations, teams can make incremental progress and deliver value in shorter timeframes. This speed-to-market advantage enables organizations to stay ahead of the competition and seize market opportunities more quickly.

Enhanced Customer Satisfaction: Agile innovation places a strong focus on customer feedback and involvement. By continuously seeking and incorporating customer input, organizations can ensure that their solutions meet customer needs and expectations. This customer-centric approach leads to higher levels of customer satisfaction and loyalty.

Improved Adaptability to Change: In today's rapidly changing business landscape, organizations need to be agile and responsive to market shifts. Agile innovation provides the flexibility to adapt to new information, market dynamics, and emerging trends. This adaptability enables organizations to stay relevant and seize opportunities as they arise.

Increased Collaboration and Engagement: Agile innovation encourages cross-functional collaboration and shared ownership. By bringing together individuals from different disciplines and empowering them to collaborate, organizations foster a sense of collective responsibility and engagement. This collaborative approach boosts creativity, enhances teamwork, and drives innovation.

Mitigated Risk and Cost Optimization: The iterative nature of agile innovation allows organizations to test and validate assumptions early on. By obtaining feedback and making refinements throughout the process, organizations can mitigate risks and reduce the likelihood of investing in solutions that may not meet market demand. This risk mitigation leads to cost optimization and improved resource allocation.

Agile innovation is a powerful approach that enables organizations to adapt, iterate, and make rapid progress in their innovation efforts. By embracing iterative processes, fostering cross-functional collaboration, emphasizing customer feedback, and embracing flexibility, organizations can foster a culture of innovation that drives continuous improvement and delivers value to customers. Implementing agile methodologies, encouraging experimentation, and leveraging agile tools and technologies further enhance the organization's ability to respond to changing market dynamics and seize opportunities. By embracing agile innovation, organizations can position themselves for success in an increasingly dynamic and competitive business landscape.

Chapter 7: Collaborative Innovation: Leveraging Partnerships and Ecosystems

Collaborative innovation involves leveraging partnerships, ecosystems, and external resources to drive creativity, share knowledge, and accelerate the development of innovative solutions. In this chapter, we explore the importance of collaborative innovation and how organizations can effectively harness partnerships and ecosystems to foster innovation and achieve sustainable growth.

The Benefits of Collaborative Innovation:

Access to Diverse Expertise and Perspectives: Collaborative innovation brings together a diverse range of partners, including suppliers, customers, startups, research institutions, and industry experts. By tapping into this network of external stakeholders, organizations gain access to a wealth of knowledge, expertise, and perspectives. This diversity fuels creativity, encourages new ways of thinking, and enhances the quality of innovation outcomes.

Shared Resources and Reduced Costs: Collaboration allows organizations to pool resources, both financial and non-financial, with their partners. By sharing the costs of research, development, and implementation, organizations can reduce their individual financial burden. Additionally, collaborative innovation enables the sharing of infrastructure, facilities, equipment, and other tangible assets, leading to further cost savings.

Accelerated Time-to-Market: Collaborative innovation can significantly shorten the time it takes to bring innovative solutions to market. By collaborating with partners who have complementary capabilities and resources, organizations can leverage their expertise, existing infrastructure, and distribution channels. This accelerates the development process, minimizes duplication of efforts, and enables faster commercialization of innovative products and services.

Risk Mitigation and Increased Resilience: Collaborative innovation allows organizations to share risks and uncertainties with their partners. By collaborating with multiple stakeholders, organizations can distribute the inherent risks associated with innovation projects. This risk-sharing approach helps mitigate the impact of failures, reduces individual exposure, and increases the overall resilience of the innovation ecosystem.

Implementing Collaborative Innovation:

Identify Strategic Partnerships: Begin by identifying potential partners that align with your organization's strategic goals and innovation objectives. Look for partners who bring complementary expertise, capabilities, and resources to the table. Consider both industry peers and non-traditional partners such as startups, academic institutions, and research organizations.

Foster a Culture of Collaboration: Cultivate a collaborative mindset within your organization. Encourage open communication, knowledge sharing, and cross-functional collaboration. Break down silos and create opportunities for employees to connect with external partners and explore collaborative initiatives. Emphasize the value of collaboration and the benefits it brings to the innovation process.

Establish Clear Objectives and Expectations: Clearly define the objectives, scope, and expected outcomes of the collaborative innovation initiative. Ensure that all partners have a shared understanding of the goals and align their efforts accordingly. Establish mechanisms for regular communication, progress tracking, and evaluation to ensure that the collaboration stays on track.

Facilitate Knowledge Exchange: Foster an environment of knowledge exchange and learning between partners. Encourage the sharing of best practices, lessons learned, and emerging trends. Leverage collaborative platforms, workshops, and joint projects to facilitate the transfer of knowledge and insights. This cross-pollination of ideas and experiences fosters innovation and strengthens the collaborative ecosystem.

Establish Effective Governance Structures: Develop governance structures and agreements that clearly outline roles, responsibilities, decision-making processes, and intellectual property rights. Establish mechanisms for resolving conflicts and addressing any potential challenges that may arise during the collaboration. Effective governance ensures transparency, trust, and a clear framework for managing the collaborative innovation process.

Embrace Open Innovation Principles: Embrace the principles of open innovation, which involve actively seeking external ideas, technologies, and solutions. Open innovation encourages collaboration and co-creation by involving external partners in the innovation process. Embrace open innovation by establishing open innovation platforms, organizing innovation challenges, or participating in industry consortia. This approach expands the pool of potential collaborators and increases the likelihood of accessing breakthrough ideas and disruptive technologies.

Benefits and Challenges of Collaborative Innovation:

While collaborative innovation offers numerous benefits, it also comes with its share of challenges. It is important to be aware of these challenges and proactively address them to ensure successful outcomes.

Trust and Alignment: Building trust among partners and aligning their objectives and expectations can be a challenge. It requires effective communication, mutual respect, and a shared vision. Investing time and effort in building strong relationships is essential to overcome this challenge.

Intellectual Property Protection: Collaborative innovation involves sharing knowledge, ideas, and sometimes even intellectual property. Organizations must establish clear agreements and mechanisms to protect their intellectual property rights while enabling knowledge sharing and collaboration.

Cultural Differences: Collaborative innovation often involves working with partners from different organizational cultures, backgrounds, and geographical locations. Understanding and appreciating cultural differences, establishing effective communication channels, and fostering a culture of inclusivity are crucial for successful collaboration.

Managing Complexity: Collaborative innovation initiatives can become complex due to the involvement of multiple stakeholders, varying agendas, and different organizational structures.

Effective project management, clear governance, and regular communication are essential for managing complexity and ensuring alignment.

Balancing Competitiveness and Collaboration: Collaborating with external partners while maintaining a competitive edge can be challenging. Organizations must find a balance between collaboration and protecting their competitive advantages to ensure a mutually beneficial partnership.

Collaborative innovation is a powerful approach that enables organizations to leverage partnerships and ecosystems to drive innovation, access diverse expertise, and accelerate time-to-market. By embracing collaboration, organizations can share resources, mitigate risks, and tap into a broader knowledge pool, leading to enhanced innovation outcomes. Implementing collaborative innovation requires building strong partnerships, fostering a culture of collaboration, establishing clear objectives, facilitating knowledge exchange, and embracing open innovation principles. While collaborative innovation presents challenges, addressing them with effective communication, trust-building, and governance structures can pave the way for successful collaborative initiatives. By leveraging the collective intelligence and resources of external partners, organizations can unleash the full potential of collaborative innovation and drive sustainable growth and competitiveness in today's dynamic business landscape.

Chapter 8: Disruptive Business Models: Reinventing Industries for Success

In today's fast-paced and ever-changing business landscape, disruptive business models are reshaping industries, challenging traditional practices, and opening up new avenues for success. These innovative approaches to conducting business have the power to redefine market dynamics, create new value propositions, and transform the way industries operate. In this chapter, we explore the concept of disruptive business models and how organizations can leverage them to reinvent industries and drive sustainable growth.

Understanding Disruptive Business Models:

A disruptive business model refers to a new way of delivering value to customers that fundamentally alters the competitive dynamics of an industry. It typically involves the introduction of innovative products, services, or processes that address unmet customer needs, create new market segments, or disrupt existing value chains. Disruptive business models often challenge established players and traditional business models by offering unique value propositions, leveraging emerging technologies, and reimagining industry norms.

Characteristics of Disruptive Business Models:

Customer-Centricity: Disruptive business models prioritize the needs and preferences of customers. They aim to create exceptional customer experiences by offering convenience, personalization, affordability, or other unique value propositions. By deeply understanding customer pain points and unmet needs, organizations can develop disruptive models that address these gaps and provide superior value.

Technology Enablers: Disruptive business models often leverage emerging technologies to drive innovation and gain a competitive edge. Technologies such as artificial intelligence, blockchain, the Internet of Things, and cloud computing enable organizations to reimagine their processes, enhance operational efficiency, and deliver new and improved solutions to customers.

Agile and Adaptive: Disruptive business models embrace agility and adaptability. They are designed to respond quickly to changing market conditions, customer demands, and emerging trends. These models enable organizations to iterate, experiment, and pivot as needed to stay ahead of the competition and seize new opportunities.

Network Effects: Disruptive business models often harness the power of network effects, creating platforms or ecosystems that bring together multiple stakeholders. By connecting customers, suppliers, and partners, these models create value through collaboration, data exchange, and network effects that amplify the benefits for all participants.

Implementing Disruptive Business Models:

Identify Industry Gaps and Unmet Needs: Conduct a thorough analysis of the industry landscape to identify gaps, pain points, and unmet needs that traditional business models have not adequately addressed. Look for emerging trends, changing customer behaviours, and technological advancements that can be leveraged to create disruptive solutions.

Embrace a Culture of Innovation: Foster a culture of innovation within the organization that encourages experimentation, creativity, and risk-taking. Encourage employees to challenge existing norms, think outside the box, and explore new possibilities. Provide the necessary resources, support, and incentives to drive innovation throughout the organization.

Embrace Emerging Technologies: Stay abreast of emerging technologies that have the potential to disrupt the industry. Evaluate how these technologies can be integrated into your business model to create new value propositions, streamline processes, and enhance customer experiences. Embrace a mindset of continuous learning and experimentation with emerging technologies.

Collaborate with Ecosystem Partners: Disruptive business models often involve collaboration with ecosystem partners, including startups, technology providers, and other industry stakeholders. Identify potential partners who can bring complementary capabilities, resources, or expertise to the table. Collaborate to co-create innovative solutions and leverage collective strengths to reinvent the industry.

Test, Iterate, and Scale: Implement a rapid prototyping and testing approach to validate the viability and feasibility of the disruptive business model. Continuously gather customer feedback, iterate based on insights, and refine the model to enhance its effectiveness. Once validated, scale the model and align organizational resources to fully exploit its potential.

Case Studies of Disruptive Business Models:

To illustrate the power of disruptive business models in reinventing industries, let's examine a few notable case studies:

Uber: Uber revolutionized the transportation industry by introducing a disruptive business model based on a mobile app platform. By connecting riders with drivers, Uber created a convenient, affordable, and efficient alternative to traditional taxi services. Its technology-enabled model allowed for seamless booking, real-time tracking, and cashless transactions. Uber disrupted the taxi industry worldwide, challenging established norms and transforming the way people commute.

Airbnb: Airbnb disrupted the hospitality industry by creating a peer-to-peer marketplace for short-term accommodations. By leveraging the sharing economy, Airbnb allowed individuals to rent out their homes or spare rooms to travellers, offering unique and personalized experiences. This disruptive model disrupted traditional hotel chains, providing travellers with more affordable and authentic accommodation options while empowering individuals to monetize their properties.

Netflix: Netflix disrupted the entertainment industry by introducing a subscription-based streaming service that revolutionized the way people consume movies and TV shows. By leveraging the power of digital distribution, Netflix eliminated the need for physical DVDs and disrupted the traditional video rental business. Its data-driven approach to content recommendations and original programming further cemented its position as a disruptive force in the industry.

Tesla: Tesla disrupted the automotive industry by pioneering electric vehicles (EVs) and leveraging advanced technologies. Tesla's innovative business model focused on designing and manufacturing high-performance, luxury electric cars while investing in a proprietary charging infrastructure. By challenging the dominance of traditional gasoline-powered vehicles, Tesla has driven the adoption of EVs and pushed the industry towards sustainable transportation.

Disruptive business models have the potential to transform industries, challenge incumbents, and create new opportunities for growth and success. By embracing customer-centricity, leveraging emerging technologies, and fostering a culture of innovation, organizations can reimagine traditional business models and develop disruptive solutions that deliver superior value to customers. Implementing disruptive business models requires a willingness to challenge the status quo, collaborate with ecosystem partners, and embrace agility and adaptability. By staying attuned to industry trends, understanding customer needs, and continuously exploring new possibilities, organizations can harness the power of disruptive business models to reinvent industries and achieve sustainable competitive advantage.

Chapter 9: Innovation Leadership: Inspiring and Empowering Change

Innovation has become a critical driver of success and competitive advantage. To foster a culture of innovation within an organization, effective leadership is essential. Innovation leaders play a pivotal role in inspiring, guiding, and empowering teams to think creatively, take calculated risks, and drive meaningful change. In this chapter, we explore the concept of innovation leadership and how it can inspire and empower individuals and teams to embrace innovation and drive organizational growth.

The Role of an Innovation Leader:

An innovation leader is responsible for creating an environment that encourages and nurtures innovation. They go beyond traditional management roles and actively foster a culture of curiosity, experimentation, and continuous improvement. Innovation leaders demonstrate the following key traits and behaviours:

Vision and Purpose: Innovation leaders articulate a compelling vision that inspires and motivates others. They establish a clear sense of purpose and communicate the importance of innovation in achieving organizational goals.

Open-Mindedness: Innovation leaders possess open-mindedness and a willingness to explore new ideas, perspectives, and possibilities. They encourage diverse thinking, challenge assumptions, and create space for unconventional ideas to flourish.

Empathy: Innovation leaders understand the needs and aspirations of their teams. They empathize with the challenges faced by individuals and create a supportive environment where people feel encouraged to share their ideas and take risks without fear of judgment or failure.

Collaboration and Empowerment: Innovation leaders foster collaboration and empower individuals and teams to take ownership of their ideas and projects. They create a culture that values teamwork, promotes cross-functional collaboration, and breaks down silos to maximize the collective intelligence of the organization.

Risk-Taking and Learning Orientation: Innovation leaders embrace risk-taking and encourage a learning orientation. They understand that failure is an integral part of the innovation process and view it as an opportunity for growth and learning. They provide support and resources to help teams experiment, learn from mistakes, and iterate on ideas.

Inspiring and Empowering Change:

Communicate a Compelling Vision: Innovation leaders must articulate a clear vision that highlights the importance of innovation and its alignment with the organization's purpose and strategic goals. By painting a vivid picture of the future, leaders inspire individuals to see the value in embracing change and taking risks.

Foster a Culture of Psychological Safety: Innovation requires an environment where individuals feel safe to express their ideas and opinions without fear of negative consequences. Innovation leaders create psychological safety by encouraging open communication, active listening, and respecting diverse perspectives. They provide constructive feedback and create a non-judgmental space where ideas can be explored and refined.

Encourage and Reward Innovation: Innovation leaders recognize and celebrate innovative ideas and contributions. They create mechanisms to encourage and reward individuals and teams for their innovative efforts. This can include recognition programs, innovation challenges, or dedicated resources for idea incubation and development.

Provide Resources and Support: Innovation leaders ensure that teams have the necessary resources, such as time, budget, and technology, to pursue innovative ideas. They advocate for innovation within the organization, securing support from stakeholders, and removing obstacles that hinder progress. They also provide mentorship, coaching, and guidance to individuals and teams, fostering their growth and development.

Lead by Example: Innovation leaders lead by example, demonstrating their commitment to innovation through their actions. They actively engage in the innovation process, participate in ideation sessions, and champion innovative projects. By showcasing their own passion for innovation and a willingness to take risks, leaders inspire others to do the same.

Innovation leadership is crucial for inspiring and empowering individuals and teams to embrace change and drive meaningful innovation. By cultivating a culture of curiosity, collaboration, and continuous learning, innovation leaders create an environment where ideas flourish and individuals feel empowered to take responsibility and actions as and when needed that will be of benefit to the business needs.

Chapter 10: Sustaining Innovation: Strategies for Continuous Growth and Adaptation

Innovation is not a one-time event but an ongoing process that organizations must embrace to thrive in today's dynamic business environment. Sustaining innovation involves developing strategies and practices that enable continuous growth, adaptation, and improvement. It requires a mindset of constant learning, agility, and a proactive approach to staying ahead of the competition. In this chapter, we explore key strategies for sustaining innovation and achieving long-term success in a rapidly changing marketplace.

Foster a Culture of Innovation:

A culture of innovation is the foundation for sustaining innovation. Organizations need to create an environment that values and encourages creative thinking, experimentation, and risk-taking. Leaders must promote a growth mindset, where failure is seen as a learning opportunity and new ideas are welcomed. By fostering a culture that supports and rewards innovation, organizations can inspire and empower their employees to continuously seek out new opportunities for growth.

Embrace Continuous Learning:

To sustain innovation, organizations must foster a culture of continuous learning. This involves promoting professional development, providing access to training programs, and encouraging employees to seek out new knowledge and skills. By investing in the development of their workforce, organizations can ensure that they have the necessary capabilities to adapt to changing market conditions and drive innovation.

Encourage Cross-functional Collaboration:

Sustaining innovation requires collaboration across departments and teams. By breaking down silos and encouraging cross-functional collaboration, organizations can tap into the diverse perspectives and expertise of their employees. This collaborative approach facilitates the exchange of ideas, sparks creativity, and promotes the development of innovative solutions that can drive continuous growth.

Develop Agile Innovation Processes:

Agile innovation processes are essential for sustaining innovation. Traditional, rigid project management approaches can hinder adaptability and slow down the innovation cycle. Adopting agile methodologies, such as Scrum or Lean, enables organizations to iterate quickly, respond to customer feedback, and adapt their strategies based on real-time market insights. Agile processes allow organizations to bring products and services to market faster, accelerating the innovation cycle and enhancing their competitive advantage.

Encourage Entrepreneurial Mindsets:

To sustain innovation, organizations should encourage entrepreneurial mindsets among their employees. This means fostering a sense of ownership, autonomy, and empowerment. Employees should be encouraged to take initiative, identify new opportunities, and pursue innovative ideas. Organizations can create innovation programs, hackathons, or innovation challenges that provide a platform for employees to develop and test their ideas, fostering a spirit of entrepreneurship within the organization.

Seek External Partnerships:

Collaborating with external partners, such as startups, universities, or industry experts, can bring fresh perspectives and novel ideas to sustain innovation. By establishing strategic partnerships, organizations can tap into external expertise, access emerging technologies, and leverage complementary resources. These partnerships can fuel innovation, open up new markets, and drive continuous growth.

Embrace Data and Analytics:

Data and analytics play a crucial role in sustaining innovation. Organizations should invest in data-driven decision-making processes and leverage analytics to gain insights into customer behaviour, market trends, and emerging opportunities. By harnessing the power of data, organizations can make informed decisions, identify areas for improvement, and develop targeted innovation strategies.

Promote a Customer-Centric Approach:

To sustain innovation, organizations must prioritize customer needs and preferences. A customer-centric approach involves understanding customer pain points, gathering feedback, and incorporating customer insights into the innovation process. By continuously engaging with customers, organizations can identify emerging trends, anticipate evolving needs, and develop innovative solutions that deliver value and enhance customer experiences.

Conclusion: Unleashing Innovation and Disruption for Lasting Business Success

In this book, we have explored the world of breakthrough strategies, unveiling the power of innovation and disruption as catalysts for business success. From the first page to the last, we have delved into the essential elements and strategies that drive transformative change and propel organizations forward in an ever-evolving marketplace. As we conclude this journey, let us reflect on the key takeaways and insights that can guide businesses on the path to lasting success.

Embrace a Culture of Innovation and Disruption:

The foundation of breakthrough strategies lies in the creation of a culture that fosters innovation, embraces disruption, and values continuous learning. Organizations that encourage curiosity, experimentation, and calculated risk-taking create an environment where breakthrough ideas can thrive. By nurturing a culture that celebrates new perspectives and rewards entrepreneurial spirit, businesses can unlock their full potential for innovation and set the stage for sustainable success.

Leverage Emerging Technologies:

In an era of rapid technological advancements, organizations must stay at the forefront of emerging technologies to drive innovation and disruption. Technologies such as artificial intelligence, blockchain, Internet of Things, and virtual reality present new opportunities to transform business models, enhance customer experiences, and optimize operations. By staying informed about emerging trends and investing strategically in technology, businesses can gain a competitive edge and capitalize on breakthrough opportunities.

Put the Customer at the Centre:

Breakthrough strategies revolve around understanding and meeting the evolving needs of customers. Customer-centricity is not just a buzzword but a critical driver of success. By deeply understanding customer desires, pain points, and behaviours, businesses can develop products, services, and experiences that truly resonate. Regularly gathering customer feedback, conducting market research, and leveraging data analytics enable businesses to make informed decisions and deliver exceptional value to customers.

Embrace Disruption and Challenge the Status Quo:

The path to breakthrough success often requires challenging the status quo and disrupting traditional industry norms. By thinking differently and questioning existing assumptions, businesses can uncover new possibilities and create transformative change. Embracing disruption means being open to change, seizing opportunities, and embracing calculated risks. It is through disruption that businesses can redefine markets, reshape industries, and position themselves as leaders of innovation.

Foster Collaboration and Partnerships:

Breakthrough strategies are seldom achieved in isolation. Collaboration and partnerships are vital in expanding horizons, accessing diverse expertise, and leveraging shared resources. By collaborating with ecosystem partners, startups, academia, and industry experts, businesses can tap into fresh perspectives, access complementary skills, and drive innovation at an accelerated pace. Through collaborative efforts, businesses can overcome complex challenges, generate novel ideas, and create breakthrough solutions.

Develop Agile and Adaptive Mindsets:

The ability to adapt and navigate change is crucial in the pursuit of breakthrough success. Agile and adaptive mindsets enable businesses to embrace uncertainty, respond swiftly to market shifts, and seize opportunities as they arise. By embracing continuous learning, agility, and resilience, businesses can stay ahead of the curve, remain competitive, and drive sustained growth. Embracing failure as a stepping stone to success and promoting a growth mindset within the organization fosters innovation and propels breakthrough strategies forward.

Stay Future-focused:

In a rapidly changing world, it is essential to keep an eye on the future. By continuously scanning the business landscape, monitoring industry trends, and anticipating customer needs, businesses can proactively identify potential disruptions and capitalize on emerging opportunities. Staying future-focused enables businesses to stay relevant, pivot when necessary, and maintain a competitive advantage in a dynamic marketplace.

As we conclude this book, we hope that the insights and strategies shared have sparked inspiration and ignited the flame of innovation within you. Embrace the power of breakthrough strategies, dare to disrupt, and unleash the full potential of your organization. The journey towards unleashing innovation and disruption for business success is not a one-time endeavour but a continuous and dynamic process. It requires commitment, adaptability, and a relentless pursuit of excellence. By applying the principles and strategies outlined in this book, you have the tools to navigate the ever-changing business landscape and drive transformative change within your organization.

Remember that breakthrough strategies are not without challenges. Along the way, you may encounter resistance, setbacks, and uncertainties. However, it is through these challenges that opportunities for growth and innovation emerge. Embrace them as learning experiences, adapt your strategies, and persevere with unwavering determination.

As you embark on your journey, keep the following key principles in mind:

Foster a Culture of Innovation: Nurture an environment that encourages creativity, curiosity, and collaboration. Foster a mindset that values new ideas, diversity of thought, and continuous learning. Create channels for idea generation, experimentation, and feedback. Celebrate and recognize the efforts and contributions of innovators within your organization.

Empower Your People: Recognize that innovation and disruption are not limited to a select few. Empower individuals at all levels of your organization to contribute their unique perspectives and ideas. Provide resources, training, and support to enable them to unleash their creativity and drive meaningful change.

Embrace Strategic Risk-taking: Breakthrough success often requires taking calculated risks. Encourage your teams to step outside their comfort zones, challenge conventions, and explore uncharted territories. Foster an environment where failure is seen as an opportunity for learning and growth. Encourage experimentation and celebrate both successes and failures along the innovation journey.

Foster Strategic Partnerships: Collaboration and partnerships can amplify the impact of your breakthrough strategies. Look beyond your organization's boundaries and seek opportunities to collaborate with external stakeholders, including customers, suppliers, academia, and industry experts. Leverage their expertise, resources, and perspectives to accelerate innovation and disruption.

Embrace Agility and Adaptability: In today's rapidly changing business landscape, agility and adaptability are essential. Be willing to pivot, adjust strategies, and seize emerging opportunities. Continuously monitor market trends, customer needs, and technological advancements. Embrace a mindset of continuous improvement and agility to stay ahead of the competition.

Invest in Technology and Data Analytics: Leverage the power of emerging technologies and data analytics to drive innovation and disruption. Embrace automation, artificial intelligence, machine learning, and other transformative technologies to enhance operational efficiency, customer experiences, and decision-making processes. Emphasize data-driven insights to gain a competitive edge and make informed business decisions.

Stay Customer-Centric: Never lose sight of your customers. Continuously seek to understand their evolving needs, preferences, and pain points. Engage in regular feedback loops, conduct market research, and use customer insights to guide your innovation strategies. Design products, services, and experiences that deliver exceptional value and meet their ever-changing expectations.

As you conclude your journey through this book, remember that innovation and disruption are not destinations but ongoing processes. Embrace a mindset of continuous improvement, adaptability, and a relentless pursuit of excellence. Be open to new ideas, challenge the status quo, and relentlessly seek breakthrough opportunities.

Unleashing innovation and disruption for business success requires dedication, courage, and a willingness to embark on uncharted paths. Embrace the journey, inspire your teams, and become a catalyst for transformative change. By implementing breakthrough strategies, you have the power to reshape industries, revolutionize customer experiences, and position your organization as a leader in the ever-evolving business landscape.

Now, armed with knowledge, inspiration, and a passion for innovation, go forth and unleash the full potential of your organization. Embrace the power of breakthrough strategies, and may your path be paved with transformative change, sustained growth, and unprecedented success. Remember that the journey towards unleashing innovation and disruption is not without its challenges, but it is through these challenges that the most remarkable breakthroughs are achieved.

Along the way, stay committed to learning and growth. Encourage a culture of continuous improvement and provide your teams with the resources and support they need to excel. Embrace feedback as a valuable tool for refinement and optimization, and use it to drive innovation forward.

As you embark on your quest for business success through breakthrough strategies, keep an eye on the horizon. The business landscape is constantly evolving, and staying attuned to emerging trends and disruptive forces is essential. Anticipate changes and be proactive in adapting your strategies to remain relevant and ahead of the curve.

Furthermore, as you navigate through the complexities of implementing breakthrough strategies, remember the importance of ethical and responsible innovation. Consider the broader impact of your actions on society, the environment, and stakeholders. Strive to create not only economic value but also positive social change.

Finally, embrace the power of leadership. As an innovation leader, inspire and empower your teams to think boldly, challenge the status quo, and push the boundaries of what is possible. Lead by example, demonstrating your unwavering commitment to innovation and disruption. Foster a culture of trust, collaboration, and inclusivity, as diverse perspectives and collective intelligence are the fuel that ignites breakthrough ideas.

In conclusion, the path to business success lies in the relentless pursuit of breakthrough strategies. It is through innovation and disruption that organizations can overcome challenges, seize opportunities, and redefine industries. By fostering a culture of innovation, embracing technology and data, staying customer-centric, and being agile and adaptable, you can navigate the ever-changing business landscape with confidence and resilience.

Let this book be your guide and source of inspiration as you embark on your journey towards unleashing innovation and disruption for lasting business success. Embrace the unknown, challenge the norms, and push the boundaries of what is possible. With determination, creativity, and a commitment to excellence, you have the power to transform your organization and shape the future of your industry.

Now, go forth and let your breakthrough strategies propel you towards unparalleled achievements. The world awaits your transformative impact.

Be sure to check out some of the other titles in this series.

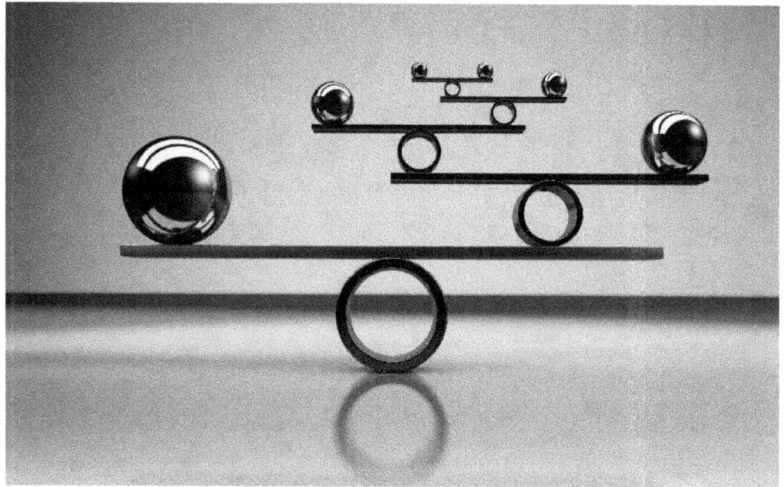